Soraya

sonnets

ANIS SHIVANI

BLACK
WIDOW
PRESS

Boston, MA

Soraya

sonnets

ANIS SHIVANI

Black Widow Press is an imprint of Commonwealth Books, Inc., Boston, MA. Distributed to the trade by NBN (National Book Network) throughout North America, Canada, and the U.K. All Black Widow Press books are printed on acid-free paper, and glued into bindings. Black Widow Press and its logo are registered trademarks of Commonwealth Books, Inc.

Joseph S. Phillips and Susan J. Wood, Ph.D., Publishers
www.blackwidowpress.com

Cover Art: *Before She Knew* by Jahna Vashti, 2010
Acrylic and spray paint on canvas
Used courtesy of the artist

Design & production: Kerrie Kemperman

ISBN-13: 978-0-9960079-7-9

Printed in the United States
10 9 8 7 6 5 4 3 2 1

for Mehnaaz

PRAISE FOR *SORAYA: SONNETS*

Cosmopolitanism has consequences for culture and ethics, as Anthony Appiah and others have shown. But it also inflects love, as Anis Shivani's effervescent Soraya sonnets attest. They are "bubble memories of the / Byzantine empire," they "have developed the language of Benares," they depict Soraya, the beloved, as the "devadasi of Dar es Salaam desert." It is ever the charge of the love sonnet to renew the meaning of the lover's declaration to the beloved that "you are the world to me." Anis Shivani's Soraya sonnets embrace that charge.

— H. L. Hix, National Book Award Finalist for *Chromatic*

Heir to the détourned music of Situationism, Anis Shivani reimagines the sonnet as a sonic excursion. Sound is sense in *Soraya*—and the linguistic tensions of Shivani's richly alliterative language invite us to accompany him "reeving through the rotten / boroughs as silent partner" in this book's wonderfully wild ride.

— Tony Trigilio, Author of *White Noise* and *Historic Diary*

Early in Anis Shivani's *Soraya*, the poet writes, "Soraya, you defy publishers in / the very building from which they issue the / ukase: umbra, shaded like political virginity, / washes over axons dialing azoic ayatollahs," and there, in four lines, you have the currency of contemporary poetry: density of histories, formal dexterity, and, put simply, serious play. The sonnets in *Soraya* clock time in service of you, reader, mapping, with remarkable sonic maneuvering, the constant sublimity of the contemporary moment. This book is intricate and wild; this book is demanding and willing to surrender; this book is "homicide in the field / house [that] has been like double fugues glazed / by qwerty purple prose."

— Nick Twemlow, Winner of the Norma Farber Award for *Palm Trees*

Soraya is a sequence of love poems where the beloved is language. The poet is thus faced with the immense catalog of the possible. What we have is a journey into the unknown; a constellation the poet composes for us, so that we may determine its coordinates. Anis Shivani continues on his path away from prescribed conformity.

— Fady Joudah, Winner of the Griffin Prize for *Like a Straw Bird It Follows Me*

ACKNOWLEDGMENTS

Many thanks to the editors of *The Account* (4), *Black Warrior Review* (78, 83, 86), *Borderlands: Texas Poetry Review* (80, 81), *Contemporary Verse 2* (23, 24, 25, 26), *Cordite Poetry Review* (41, 42), *Everyday Genius* (31, 32, 33), *Ink Node* (38, 67, 79, 92, 98), *The Journal* (61, 62, 63), *Mudlark* (12, 13, 14, 15, 16, 17), *The Nervous Breakdown* (18, 19, 20), *Omniverse* (1, 72), *Phoebe* (45, 47, 48, 49, 50), *Volt* (25, 26, 28), *Waxwing Literary Journal* (34, 35, 36), *Western Humanities Review* (64, 65, 66, 68, 69), and *Whiskey Island* (43, 44), where many of these sonnets originally appeared.

Thanks to Dave Brinks, Harvey Hix, Fady Joudah, Jay Parini, Kevin Prufer, Tony Trigilio, Nick Twemlow, and Franz Wright for their outstanding support. And to Adam Robinson, Michael Joseph Walsh, Tyler Mills, Gillian Conoley, Elizabeth Doran, William Hastings, Peter Krok, Ifeanyi Menkiti, Rusty Morrison, Caroline Rash, and William Slaughter for encouragement while I was writing this book. Many thanks to the artist Jahna Vashti for lending her lovely painting for the cover image, and deep gratitude to Kerrie Kemperman for her wonderful work in making this the most beautiful book it could be. Thanks to Mehnaaz for the supreme gifts of time and love.

Above all, thanks to Joe Phillips and Susan Wood for giving this book a home at a press whose illustrious authors I have always idolized; this is a dream come true for me.

1.

Heavy water, Soraya, hectares of lithium,
your angry locusts past the seventeenth
year of pining, while your carnival mermans,
we—mercurial, mentholated, mephitic natives—
revive the rhythm of breathing in rhumba,
rewrite the vitreous record books to void,
sprockets of hope to your sprouting reich,
each of the thirteen colonies tone-deaf.
We, chimeriad of Sorayas in chilly cranes,
measure childbearing like faquirs out in
fanzines, live family trees hanging gimpily
on the lobes of *pad, pat, bad, bat* phonemes.
Secret shoppers are their own sect of spook,
tiebreaking tutors whisking voiceless vodka.

2.

God's splintered trireme, like oysters at sea,
troubadour eyes handed to us in trousseaus,
stromal streets, Soraya, metabolize kempt
Devanagari hindquarters, gussets of wind-
channeled gurneys, gypsum in dogs' breath.
Grand dame of grammalogues, it is de jure
in your demesne to delay colorfast fatigue,
cartwheel past case-hardened caryatids:
entablature carved by your cassette hands
amid ruins of cartilage and gross cassocks
of that single color, placenta, pulling strings
as though public servants were blogging
biomes, occurring naturally like birdcages.
I am bisque, Soraya, to black bison in stone.

3.

Stoneware cannot stomach, cannot stomp
over topologies of abstract secrets, tongue
and groove, Soraya, you defy publishers in
the very building from which they issue the
ukase: umbra, shaded like political virginity,
washes over axons dialing azoic ayatollahs.
Belle of the ball, upon the bending belvedere,
summer sets to caucuses of hoodoo palms.
Trembling at the lectern, lean jabberwocky
issuing like hors d'oeuvres for horse-trading,
I, Soraya, marquise in maroon, mascot to
masons, denounce gag rules in gay ghettos,
the lifespan of pigmentation piercing my
arches and piers, and no more pillow talk.

4.

Blood of descendants, Soraya, platinum
graphs of Polynesian math, somewhere
in the darwinian islands polymaths' braille
brains loosen lotus notes, lost for words.
Coloratura saturates democracy taking root
in ashes, aspidistra assigned to blow-dried
circadian dividers of the island. Obloquy
favors ocarina made of occidental mouth-
piece. Phoenix rising from phosphorous
doge telephone, Soraya, your philippic
this examined morning snowing letters
and business, sniffing out the soft clam
wherein I solemnize solfège of typhoon
typewriters. Tweedy, our twilight-fused
twins, twisting in the wind on twig beds.

5.

Porcelain pop art we pontiffs of cayenne
abdicate, Soraya, your placebo relations,
poor like broken hips, etiolated as eunuchs
of ripening animal behavior, ethicists of
eulogy, every last one of us. And eureka!
Said safflower to same-sex samovar, scrap
circumlocutions clambering in civic mud,
bagatelles of piano beams benefit whales.
Stylus composing subjunctive styrene
sublimations, I procured, Soraya, from
the pivoting movement of timberline,
wolf timescale, tingle of trade winds,
variola decoupled from decoration day,
cofferdams so cold cognomens freeze.

6.

Gateway to fuchsin reclamations, front-
page frost covering the first fruit of archaic
wombs, Soraya, fuguist of the gang futon,
gazetteers remain geographical indexes,
gay in Gauguin's art after the sermons:
gather me in your strip of chic Gaullism.
Hispaniola whose hispid history infringes
like jimson weeds to the jingle of joule
effects: afterward, in the Kleenex silence
of knife-throwing klephts, we know the
bottom in two half hitches, knuckling
under lentigines caused by liege homage,
as your nettle rash, Soraya, netizen of
neutrality, nibbles at my chrome niche.

7.

Scutage we paid, Soraya, scuttering past
scrolls of Sheela-na-gig, slantwise our
congratulations at spline curves spoiling
thanatalogy's thank-you letters, thank
you Thar desert, thank you thanksgiving,
thank you theater-in-the-round: thegns
trotting out vagal utopias, honing wedge
luminaria, promising lamia-pitying lambs.
Lampoon that lets us drink to nasal refrain,
lambda signifying diminutive mezza voce
we reserve, Soraya, for minyans Miró of
the spiky mirrors held in Miocene nights,
your Miranda satellites obeying obbligatti
to the omega point, onomasts in ink pads.

8.

We paddle toward the moon's packing
density, Soraya, packframes impacting
Paganini pizzicati encased in edges,
our past relativity resiled for recherché
readerships: chat rooms equal unfaithful
rhymes, Chechen carousels, carpet sharks,
carrion beetles, Carolingian carpentry
(belle-époque bottoms out the bell curve).
You make me feel ancient, an ancient
pair of jeans, and did you steam it open,
your bag of anchorites, Anaximenes's
flat earth argued through arterial change,
Soraya, champak trusting emotive charas,
chanticleers rousing antiphonal dams.

9.

Old clothes, old sofa, an eyesore that old barn,
odalisques framed in off-color perinatal oeils-
de-bouef, Soraya, omphalos of muscle grunge:
Calliope, Clio, Erato, Euterpe, Melpomene,
Polyhymnia, Terpsichore, Thalia, Urania,
formal afflatus con brio, con moto, crescendo
mutating toward my pageboy noyade, niveous
Nixon knocking nouveau nizams observing
noumena inhering in nowcasts. Soraya, of
late the prismatic privy council has probed
scumbles resembling scurvy grass, while I
segregate stemwinders from stenotopic steps,
démodé escapades suited to vintage Eskimos,
prune oculists' offenses to insurgent justice.

10.

The Cartesian product, Soraya, of the Oedipal
complex, cascara obtained in Casco Bay,
chartered charm school whose elastic fiber
unravels at the first mention of Eisenstein:
montage eightfold electrostatic, El Greco's
elongations like software prone to hara-kiri,
Hanoverian hangmen tasking the minor axis
of hazardous pornography, technique of tedium.
Mellowly, Soraya, draw out the melanin
infecting my new engrams, memetic traces
coursing through known coups de théâtre,
while Courbet chips at *Burial at Ornans*:
to be a boy watching my mother castrating
cinquefoil, twice the circuit Circe restored.

11.

Egrets, their distinctive eidos, like exhibits
on ego trips, ETA dear effluent snake
when fioritura runs out of fipple flute,
the Finlandization of my favor high-
pitched enough to alter the genotype
neither of us, Soraya, was born with.
Lohengrin carried away in the longhair
boat, longitudinal waves sparking jumps
lost without hipsters, lords spiritual and
second-caused, we meet like secateurs
greeting the year at the time of sowing,
Soraya a sack of secondary feathers,
my ska sizable in sizzle, all the sit-up
situationists awaiting endless sitzkrieg.

12.

Novena inferno, Soraya, pessimism bound
in linguistics' lingam style, incunabulum
overlaid with blocks of Serb program code,
reed organs reeking of cancerous reflexes,
while the ronds de jambes our Röntgen new-
borns perform to livid Roman candles awaken
tetralogies of higher criticism: Dada, daddy
dactyls, Daedalus's volcanic dab hands.
Dacha in Dachau, Soraya, the experimental
four hundred migrating to the forty-ninth
parallel, loaded with founder effects, jolies
laides speaking Ladino to knock me up,
while the mahdis of Mahayana mail-bomb
paralegals inhabiting hippy-dippy paradors.

13.

The day you tricked out my big garden of
primate marigolds, Soraya, prime mover
among pricks and eyelids, your priestcraft
like the inductors of Indore, I, combat-
fatigued, broadbrushed britzka seating
broken arrows and the tenants of Brontë,
announced the brotherhood of dorados,
dot-com doting upon dormouse douanes.
Max passed the ball back at the coffee
klatch, Soraya, lookalike to St. Bernards,
sake in hired porcelain, exoskeletons
worthy as exit polls, ex libris Cosimo de'
Medici, Cecil B. De Mille, Bette Davis,
all who hindered the Hindenburg Line.

14.

Strange full-mouthed ladies tweet Fulani
to destroy the Mata Hari fulcrum, Soraya,
full employment ever the fugato of bores,
punji sticks killing novice homosexual
punks required to observe purist purdah,
while pundits of the Punic Wars exert
their fortunes in Sedona's sepoy mutiny,
seraglios draped in stations of the cross.
Serape you wear, Soraya, buttoning your
lips, nets ayurvedic Ayeshas whose
axis of pain in the afterlife is illegal
even on the left bank. Left-footed legatees
embark on jelly phaetons toward petting
zoos, play dates with platinum blondes.

15.

Chauffeuse, vetchling, chatelaine in the
baggage check area, your castanets ring,
Soraya, like Cassius during assassination.
I cast lots with your mind's routers, bow-
sprit slowing the vessel down, bacchant
who invaded Babur from Oxus to Patna,
those arrhythmic arrière-pensées you know
like the arthroscope recently in my preen
gland. Ventricles formed in Venn diagrams,
or cerclage binding Cerberus to centrist
historiography, hodiernal hobbyists in
hobble skirts, ourselves, Soraya, halving
the other half, otaku hiding in the house,
Oudh's oubliettes rained out for readers.

16.

Cortés, whose coruscant cortex cosmographs
denote fiercely among the Comanche, come
down from the combustion chamber, Soraya
awaits with caffè latte, caftans from Cairo,
PTA abiding by Parkinson's law, parfait
approved by communal parishad. Parergon
roles misconduct Valkyries toward valets
curtsying to bring down the curtain on trans-
lation. Bon voyage, Soraya, bonesetter
to the booboisie, gather your bonobos to
match the small purse: Arabists, like turista,
involving hot air or steam, tunnel-visioned,
my thirty-one-day zip codes to the zodiac,
jumping through downloaded dove trees.

17.

Farouche dream, farthingale around mungo,
dream of fartlek disabling the dash of fasces,
Soraya, peyote buttons fall in love with your
stepson, leaving behind black swan letters:
phallic pews, Petrarchan weeknights, chirpy
chlamydia, bezique bhangra, roadworthy
jury, we recently scored the genre's first hit.
(Our kairos needs Karbala in kangaroo courts.)
Childproof cove, blank check when we cherish
chevaliers brittle like Broca's area, or band
of aphasia, Soraya unmake us, nihilist nikah
nonexistent. Nil desperandum! The nineteenth
hole in Nineveh flowers in late October, like
daisies fluffy for white clouds in flugelhorns.

18.

Pilgrimage to Peters projection, petit jeté
pulsating to double acrostics, Soraya, kiss
me in Kipling's kiosk, crores of Coltranes
colonize the code: colophon we, color-
blindedly, drew with crayons, is bouffant,
minus all the blue notes we penciled for
the blushers and the Aurangzeb-austere
au pairs, the raspings of Aristotle's lantern.
Amen corner is ambient in ambergris music,
impatiens grow old in impacted craters,
Soraya, infibulations in India ink ignite
overthrown ikebanas appearing illiquid.
Protomartyrs Prester John pressed into
service now moralize for morning gifts.

19.

Your tarantism, Soraya, like the cavorting
of tarpon in pterosaur-infected tarns, acts
to publicize the riding cymbals of Tarsus:
trouvères preceding Proudhon and Trotsky
have fallen in trouble with weeping willows,
lunette lungs lurch toward errant Galatea
brought to life in galley proofs, and knight
bachelors knit ogee arches in Mumbai.
(He taught me Reichian emotional release.)
Your viperfish vipassana, Soraya, hires
my high-resolution image as Hindutva's
dosshouse, cryopreserved crystal net
recording the cosmographies of corsairs,
busking on the sidewalks of business cycles.

20.

Grown for its spurred flowers, attracting
butterflies, my valency, Soraya, is vatic
crepitation, cretic crib-biting, crenulated
head to Bandaranaike's banana plug.
The bane of the decorator is the narrow
hall, dove gray in downfall, dowager's
hump causing failures in Ishihara tests.
Ischemia surrounds the island arc grown
old like Islamabad. Costermongers cough
at Soraya's council of war, cotton-picking
minute tickling my cost-effective costard.
Clavate lesbianism, peregrine grass (cum
grano salis) is poison gas, pointless point
spread for poker-faced pointing devices.

21.

Flemish flesh, the pleasures of, the way of
all, on the bones, its sins, making it crawl:
the side wounds of fleur-de-lis, Soraya,
flavescent when we flayed Melchizedek,
who melded palsy and personal injury
perturbations. Reiki, in this reign of terror,
reimburses anabasis advancing through
analysis of Agartala's afterglow once the
market has set. Accouchement, in Accra's
accredited pulp cavities, results, Soraya,
in brochettes immune to broccoli rabe.
Wearing bengaline, Berenice, her hair in
beret, bends my ear with barnacles whose
acid jazz awakens Avalon's awkward age.

22.

Coprolalia down to its nude graphemes,
cinerarium where cinephiles circle dance
around the funhouse where you, Soraya,
quaff quintals of quirky query languages,
my paisley pagoda sleeve ever the hoax
to your hobbits enslaved by hobnails,
having finished the quadrivium qawwali-
lodged, logarithms logjammed in Locrian
mode. Dyarchy of dybbuk-born dystrophy
apportions a priori apsaras frogkicking
the frontispiece, Soraya, our frowst-
bitten frontmen, Komodo dragons, kraft
kraken, prescinding publication of April
trade figures, rataplan to rat-bite fever.

23.

Excluding pork, shellfish, milk, and rattan,
we rationalize tanagers tanning in the tonga,
Soraya, tam-tam rousing gravid tamagotchi.
I collect utility knives vaccinating me against
mare clausum, nocturnal black margates slow
off the mark against marsh gas, chilling us to
our marrow when we schedule the schlubs.
(Statistics bear out subglacial suffragism.)
In our three-day truce, Soraya, trudging past
tropics of trumpet vines, umber encryptions
endear us to the bricolage of painted junk.
I open wide the breviary at the Bridge of
Sighs, brewmaster to ingravescent ingénues,
inhuming red admirals in sedilia sediment.

24.

Seedsnipes see me though minority deception,
subjacent to letters of marque you granted,
Soraya, when we fell in the subclass of bench-
warmers in Belshazzar's palace walls: bimah
below arabesque solutions, araneids crawling
into Howrah's howling hubble constants, hum
of iambus languid like ibizan hounds, buildup
to Caligula's calefacients, calendar of worms.
Callaloo, our life and limb, light sensitive rho,
rhapsodes flying like rhea among rhomb titans
and rhesus monkeys burring the soft left
ridges around bush pilots you hired, Soraya,
for bavardage of Ptolemaic origin: swindle
swept-up in the tempo of a bag of sweets.

25.

Tzarina's tzedakah, like typhus-postponed
tyrant flycatchers whose typology among
the Tzotzil is set to smart bombs going off
at the smirch of smart quotes, Soraya, trove
of catalogues raisonnés, you resemble only in
ausculation's austral sounds. Bend sinister,
auteur of nicotiana, we are but thrifty tokens
of unteachable agronomy, Ahriman's aigrette.
Acephalous paisans, Soraya, wetbacks to
Werner's syndrome, wrinkle your write-in
candidacy to be wharfinger among trembling
trees of life: tremolo producing earth tremor,
I touch your lethean partition as amicus curiae,
shakti shaky as shale oil, shagging the mask.

26.

Soraya, devadasi of Dar es Salaam desert,
my detached retina has lately been destitute
of cynosure. I was the queen of Polaris of all
eyes, Cymbeline among untorn cyclists, cacao
feeding caddis worms, cachexia's metabolic
cadet. Now I am laid like a rutile cable car
along tracks of sabers, sabbatarian in sailor
suit, sclerotium speaking up for spear grass.
Do not abide, says Soraya, weather stations
whose bouleversement, on boutique nights,
is multitasking's municipal neoclassicism;
do not, dear nematocyst, neophyte of Nejd,
get on the rice burner to trouble tropologies
suited to trout lilies and true-false tests.

27.

Emerging from nowhere, trophy wife
troubleshooting tumbledown tuileries,
tuk-tuk in a tumult of tungsten hearts,
Soraya, tudor rose earnest like eaglet
in my underwater earhole, diaspore
applauds defloration on degree day.
Dehradun defies political frost's poste
restante possessive pronouns, Soraya,
so embark on postils like rhizomorphs
deluded, like rheboks running repairs
for runways in Runnymede. My rupiah
feeds Silicon Valley's silent semicolons,
antique Sikhs of slang, slag heaps of slave-
state touch-me-nots, tout le monde.

28.

The wedding of hive bees, HIV-positive doxy,
Soraya, draft dodger to dozens of souteneurs,
is nothing like our down-to-earth draggle-
tailed doxologies. We pair paintboxes paid
for by Pahlavi's pains, paladins of paleo-
pathology, rich like jinrickshas riding up
rift valleys in the Sierpinski triangle: sigil
as significant as Shiva's situs inversus
after the first sitz bath. Do you remember
data gloves? Darkling beetles obscure the
age of racism for Dasein dashing about.
Soraya, dare me to swim the Dardenelles,
my date of birth is suspicious susurrus,
hardly a punctilio on the swage block.

29.

Sutlej, Panjnad, Chenab, swag of suzerain
clothes, the suspense kills combfish clones,
Soraya's coma, Comaneci's colza (drape come
to nothing), carousel to arak, aquifer aging
like aphorisms of apologia: akrasia less
noticeable than albatross in an air sac,
rescue à la carte for ablative absolutes,
muons from Muqdisho putting a price on
murrain. Catalexis in casual waters lasts
only as long as equipotent palladia guard
Soraya's palatine tegmentum, explosive like
Te Deum in exultation, telamones offering
the flag of truce to undocumented undines,
flagitious flâneurs necking flamingoes.

30.

Akhenaton, uninvited wedding guest, akimbo
for akashic traffic control, Soraya's alabaster
cheek lifts your aitchbone to carob tree of
caring: cargo cult, dulce de leche, interferon
akindle, kingfisher's english craft and kinesis,
petty cash after love for three oranges, coal-
mining city for projection television, rough
trade among stewbums, roués, spiny lobsters.
Weasel weatherman of ethernet endings, like
wazirs in Brazzaville brawling for a break in
the traffic, for euphuism's Eurasian ingress,
Soraya is Akbar's insolvable instauration,
pagan padlock near Rajbari, sprezzatura's
entourage, spring beauty to square waves.

31.

Correspondents swayed by craggy coxcombs
in cowtowns across saltine craters, Soraya,
know our salt lick has been volatile for years,
search engines having collided with turtles
and urchins climbing the sea wall as planets
characteristic of stress: Shri shrew-mole
asked me last night about the showdown,
and I was shroud-laid, shrunk in my shtetl.
Kashruth in Kathiawar, Soraya, involving
AK-47s frozen like katabatic Karajan,
kapellmeister rising like a flèche among
the flecks of campanile sunshine, our flax
flautist whose drogue parachute droops
in song, town droogs daydreaming of jobs.

32.

Dateline Karachi: checksum, checkered flag
of chemical abuse, casting bread upon the
waters of laughter, the bravura of bilboes,
binary operation upon the beach buggy of
my favorite bawd, while you, Soraya, bead
of hijra, high holiday leaping over Hilbert
space, monofilament for monition, fjord
between my legs, discover the fissionable
rush basket, my earphone to earth. Soraya,
the monkey on my back is a mongoloid
nitwit, Nkrumah's noetic no-fault prize,
drinking palm wine, Pandarus panicking
me to monoglot cycling. I am left mucking
about the misprision of my mulatto rule.

33.

We were spellchecking the Giza Sphinx
for Spenserian stanzas, Soraya, spermaceti
drenching spicy candles originating in our
spine. Spin doctors came out in touring
cars, unloading touchwood, yanking off
toupees and prayer shawls, precipitating
fetuses knocked by ferules. You make me
a diorama in a field of camping dinosaurs,
intermezzo in crocket. Crones hoping to
die, Soraya, are bespoke units, precentors
whose prebendary we never begrudge.
Still, the pratique you worked hard to get
is never immune to revision, even Quet-
zalcoatl abandoning mornings to quinine.

34.

I am stevedore to unknown sterilized silver
chemists, stickler for stigmaria shocked
into being by text-wrapped sticky Thalia.
Soraya, tetrarch of mash note terreplein,
you reinforce the rules of kriegspiel with a
light hand, my kyrie spreading like kudzu
regardless of Kshatriya boundaries. (Kulaks
always knew just enough Kremlinology.)
Laic Lok Sabha performs long division
over necessary neckcloths, the Near East
a near gale, the revolt of Soraya's ullage
a felix culpa curving to the bend of massifs.
Carrier pigeons alight on carousels facing
labor camps lit by Lahori lacquerwork.

35.

The corpus delicti of our long separation
is recorded in ladder tournaments among
ladies who lunch, stays hung up in the print
queue, Soraya, shadow play in Java and
Bali sheathing my textualism when I
violate the skaldic rule of informal union.
Hematocele collects in empty Helmand,
the mural crown abandoned to murine
musclemen. The stage door, boustrophedon
sprawl to austere aureate anharmonicity,
leads Soraya to the altar, occult shekinah
illumined by shell companies and vinyl
hung in the usual way, wealthy zodiac
zoned to the campus site of camisoles.

36.

Cheatgrass where the colorists among the
beau monde beat back the lone surviving pietà
of me holding you like a prosecuting infant,
Soraya, echoes spondaic theanthropy,
the truth condition under which I wait up
for the Wagner tuba to wail around air
raids. (The wave state lighting the wagon
train might as well be Wahhabis on strike.)
Yokozuna burst open their loanwords at
the moment when isomorphic hard drives
freeze along the frontage of our septal
matrilineality. I swear upon the codpiece,
Soraya, to snuff the establishment Essenes
whose ecbolic eclogues throb with courtesy.

37.

Salvage yard for scholiasts in consensual
scatter diagrams, Soraya, couturière to
bigeminy's conscience clause, conscription
in the breweries of graph paper personifies
the sea-green spine-chilling sweet spot
in our tea garden. I couldn't tear myself
away from timbering in a time capsule
washed up at the megabit birth canal.
Soraya, matutinal mausoleums aside, how
do maunds of Maxwell's demons, mayflies
in private practice, affect the prisoner's
dilemma you hold off for Lumière's lucky
projector? The lumpenproletariat is midway
to the middle kingdom's pathetic fallacy.

38.

Patch reef our morning paternoster landed
us on, like paupers excluded from pavane
among the patriots of desktop publishing,
describes, Soraya, the indigo Munch we
mummified for the multitudes: rus in urbe,
red channel to sagittal crest, Sadducees
betting on safety razors, the sago palm
inside our salaryman's Saladin caste mark.
To foretell your blancmange prepuce, my
Rawalpindi razzia ended in kill zone razzle-
dazzle. I know, Soraya, the June bug juku,
I know Houdini's hourglass late hours, I know
gynecoid gypsies whose ground effect is
gracile government, silk surplus on tablets.

39.

Maharajah playing magnolia mah-jongg,
mock moon whose parallax lotus bites
we bear in letterpress silence, Soraya,
Simeon's simcha in hindsight was silver
age to the leaves of simple time, and so
we ticked over to tourmaline horizons,
we touched the townies to pay up to
the golconda of diastole high days.
Scuncheon defoliated by degrees of
freedom, until your fons et origo, Soraya,
is folk tale no more, is neither food pyr-
amid nor folium in the Folies Bergère,
surely not the etiology of the Eton collar
empurpled with cupfuls of cupidity.

40.

Graticule we theorized in the meltwater
past missiology, misrule we recorded in
talk of politics, Soraya's rectrix ruling
the truce this year of warm-up venery.
In the new wars of the roses (winepress
in the compulsory chapel) character
recognition instructs Durga juries about
points of law, cabriole leg's seiza pose.
When we, Soraya, shocetim archetypes,
calculate the azimuth between tangent
and tangent (the precinct of shocking
pink, electric shock), we find brumal
snakes powdered in sugar, brush fires
seen through autofocus, verbs in apnea.

41.

Visions of the louse, lotus-eater in Louvre,
midinette's MIDI the missing link to your
mistrial, Soraya, destructive halogen truth
burdening my Recife recollections: squaws
looking for square meals in the thunderous
textbooks of erotology, dust-delivered
atoms of mise en scène where playboys
reach secretariats of intelligence, wounded
by rabbit's foot. Rabbinical quipu, our
quintet of hermit crabs taking over the
ghat leading down to ghibelline ghetto,
Soraya, we all cheat on the exacta, propped
up by the dry misericord, package tours
ending in nightly finger-of-god juju.

42.

Daddy longlegs comes to me in a czarina's
cretaceous dream, pointing out Soraya's
battle-hardened crepe de chine indicia,
and the public address system explodes
in the self-involved night with spicules
of perversion: the fornax pesthouse is full
of outspoken pacifists, outpatients in space
marked by mushrooming magic lanterns.
In an enchained gravure, I emigrate on
difficult nights toward your besieged
delta, Soraya, conservationist of energy,
cloud hopping toward pianola closure.
Your curvature of lithic démenti supports
the little people's curse of the glass jaw.

43.

Martial eagles, martinets who were never
country cousins, concentrate their graphic
comstockery on concertos led by Punjabi
punkettes: rack rent extorted by raconteurs
whose second childhood is like Soraya's
forgotten memory bank, axis of symmetry
rotated until the capriccio fossilizes into
integers of subordination. Young palominos
are limping with the acceleration of lineage,
limited-edition anesthesia scattering their
madrigal main page. Soraya, melodeon of
small defeats, your nightriders are fat,
like Father's Day, like the fauborgs of
Fatima, fer de lances' feminine rhymes.

44.

Feme sole, mending your ferial fences,
doomed your fermata, the flood lighting
your itinerate ivy, mala fide mosque,
most high mother wit, moth-eaten I
pamper palmetto motifs, Soraya's palp
debuting the Decameron's coping saw.
My monkey jacket's monocarpic wailing
is a puzzle tree, tree with spiny scales,
necklace of spores. Rodin's readerly
reactions, his brittle bone disease in
broad daylight, kayak to Kepler's laws,
kestrels hovering over Jhansi's kosher
koine, and Soraya a restricted kraal,
orphan drug to Orphism's orthodoxy.

45.

I believe in licking riot grrrl power beads.
I believe in ring-around-a-rosy to move
the Mensheviks' frozen mercury. I believe,
Soraya, in Roman candles whose eidetic
effusion kills the licensed goose. I believe
in rodomontade among splashy waterfalls,
cold water the spitting image of Thomism.
(Thoth, messenger of pins, screw the waves
with gray snaps of Valentino.) Whose voo-
doo voters volunteer most often for ex
cathedra evulsions? Whose ewe neck,
Soraya, exceeds the prayer wheel's quack
oscillations? Whose quantum of shivering
wrecks the form-fitting snows of Shiraz?

46.

Frescoes which blow in like frequent
breezes from the exercise book containing
our common exergue, fidus Achates,
Soraya, fifth wheel of fame, field of
Daphnis, invent for me a dance card
among danaids, mock butterfly damping
the damask origin of bitter rot. Bivouac
on the bisexual mountain is diagrammed
in stalled droshkies. Soraya, conjure
woman fraternizing with libertine congas
(the Golgi apparatus of poetry dying
since the Cape of Good Hope), accuse
me of being gonzo gonfalonier flunking
the life guard's Holocene instinct to save.

47.

Pink lido, cone of feathers in sea lavender,
ducks quaking with the nettle of passing
miles, stool pigeons from Elysium knowing
all about embolisms among freemartins
running out of gasoline or epic sphene:
thallus you formed, Soraya, of histories
of encaustic empire-building, unwinds
like crewel work in the blindness of the
Mercalli scale. Bushido's forest rules,
bursitis in Arcadia, archangels' army of
anamnesis, all that goes into Soraya's
analects of the juddering Judas kiss:
in the end Judith saves nothing but
Meerut's lucky dip of immovable fruit.

48.

Lucknow, your bearded ludic sum of eyes,
megalithic medusoids of purblind need,
Soraya's punitive damages are the dark
matter Deirdre's paintbox wisely ignores.
Prosthetic news of the clastic cordon sani-
taire reminds Calliope of the metronome
demolishing the mezzanine code of
mortality, morning glory spread-eagled
before midday. Détente among dicrotic
memorials is like the phony war Soraya
enforces, meniscus composed to maps
of rope ladders ending in root directories,
sieve plate of my sigma cross signed like
sympathetic magic on the traffic island.

49.

Closed tragus, trahison des clercs on the
ski trail to the trading post, the gray parrots
imprisoned by Soraya having spoken of the
great divide, de haut en bas minor orders
obstructing their own orthogenesis toward
Stanislavski's standing waves: threnody
which comes over the transom like tumulus
written out of the vacuum's vade mecum.
I ascend the utility vehicle of counterattack,
pericardium pulsing to aboriginal hope,
Soraya's abscission absent from the glottal
stop, abreaction as wide as camera lucida
mounted on camion visible like overdue
heriot, coheir to perilune bottles of coraline.

50.

Laudanum smuggled in the minaudière you
panegyrized, Soraya, exurban primo uomo,
diphthong among cottiers, like brisk coulisses
in the landscape of beignets, befouls the air
of arithmetic. Atmospherics aside, Mount
Athos welcomes your athletic atman, atop
the atelier of homeopathy's least-squares
moxie: homology in which you reappear
as fainéant corkage, displaced person to
the ten-headed demon king, ravelin set
to the cantos of black-market bristlings.
Daily I perceive curvatures in graymail,
Soraya, the net present value of neuroleptics
reformed to meet the camber of our IDs.

51.

Many passing bells have rung in these pigeon
months since we conducted the passeggiata
along our peace sign's elliptic curve: pas de
deux for Soraya's reserve bank, sweet violet
producing pergola blues from the unsayable,
passel of Elizabethan sonnets, on to El Paso
couchette of rainforest light traveling as
probative Julian calendar. Jumble of juliet
caps pulse through the pumice artery of my
punching bag for Soraya, rose of Jericho
stamping me with intaglio cylinders, rot-
gut chafing the windows of macaronic
lyrics: in our privy chamber grapnel sunk
in mothercraft, mandamus to yield milk.

52.

Route march at last routine for sloe-eyed
slippery chasseurs, divestment from all of
Soraya's proclitic rhythm and blues, the
stylolite of endangered fountains a short
drive from contraception. Pasquinade we
performed in rubicund Pashto, addressing
the chalaza that binds us to the chambers of
guilt, was another brick in the veneer of the
mushroom cloud. Music videos in the late
comedy of nosology arrive like blind terriers
scribbling on the notepads of Soraya's
retinoblastoma. Sweet-and-sour reticulum,
graveyard shift for fuglemen of the left,
I have swallowed the forceps of first causes.

53.

The two Sorayas like clinker bricks dead
in Ormazd's business park, the rain dance
clientele erasing beaches in Rajasthan's
SGML shackles, sexfoil clerisy clear-eyed
about maverick payloads in mescaline skies.
Note clusters roam around the gay flutes
of nostalgie de la boue, our nosocomial
off-message illnesses like aged oil slicks.
Old man, your beetle spots olivaceous in
punch cards, pull-quotes from repo men
fill the fifth generation's feu de joie with
Soraya's lèse majesté miniaturism. Mine
shafts are conduits for catalectic evangels:
monocles, compos mentis, blunt like butter.

54.

Quasi contract imposed by the stations of
poetic license, Soraya's humor, periodic
function of perjury among Menes's glossy
periwinkles, periphrastic syntax ranging
over the days of awe, helix of meltwater
holidays: ethnocide on brigantine meme
sailing toward metic resurrection plants,
ecdysis revealing ecce homo crowned
with echolalia. Ebonized constative we
consiglieri loaned to res publica, like
Soraya's bureaux de change scattered
at the stake: burnt bushes, glass in the
bayou, beacon of Askhabad's ashcan
school of slums, askesis of memory.

55.

Metritis afflicting Manet's honor system,
if not mange among the roots of mania,
the roadshow, Soraya, whose secret
service is second in line only to tattlers
at tattoo ceremonies: teachers college
at which the fellows' ticky-tacky prose
gives utopian usherettes ideas of failed
uxoricide. Uttar Pradesh's vacuole heat
allows periodic lateralization of Soraya's
crab canon located among message-
switching mahants. Mestiza of neume,
nevus marks me as an exclave of deodars.
Defenestration of objets trouvés by glass
damsels of conjuncture is paynim's right.

56.

With Giorgione's glabrous ease, Soraya
gives me up for Jamshedpur's janissaries
in metonym's paper bag. The returning
officer approves revenant genres in revenge
tragedies, rosicrucians in the syllable-
timed ROTC permitting synarchy among
heteroecious firstborns. Fireblight scorches
the collateral firmament of coleopterists
in conference. Hessian boots sound in the
moonless hexagonal machinery like cat-
amites consuming bêches-de-mer in ashy
willingness. Overnight, Soraya's asiatic
breeze comes ashore like art paper blown
up anonymously for the answering service.

57.

Antemortem, instructions from Soraya were
antenna for inroads into sheitels' inoperative
texture. Later, entropy's entourage, in propria
persona, turned out to be clothed in clouds,
clozapine guitars playing chaste pederasty:
peep show carried out to the rhythm method,
peepul burnt in cosmology's drinking songs,
carriole taking us to the Ouija board of our-
selves in ottava rima. Uruborus drawn like
Urdu in cut-up cyanide, Soraya's cutlass
sprang around my blue pencil in ribbons
of somatic edits: corsage of entoptic verse
pinned in ephemeris time, epigones' musk
of musica ficta saturating the homestretch.

58.

On the home front, homicide in the field
house has been like double fugues glazed
by qwerty purple prose. The Franklin stove's
death certificate awaits in fretwork of
frijoles, frangible welding between sharks
frightened of their island shadows. Soraya,
the Hooghly hook-and-ladder trucks' jeu
d'esprit reaches the hippogriff's hindmost
hands. I took Seconal last night to make
room for the sea robins. The searchlight
showed me in possession of season tickets
to graveyards overrun by gay parrots. I
flew into Soraya's digital chorister, quinine
on my lips, falciform face of ice climbing.

59.

Ichneumon, sunlight's primitive beast,
I practice raja yoga among cats and dogs
attuned to the dogman's handle. Dead
from the neck up, ciné-vérité circumvents
canonicity among makers of peace signs.
Ratamacue within Rasputin's earshot,
Soraya's raspberry exchange, shul at the
shutter speed of cartilage, cascades in
the public domain. I find pubescence
among enemies of Shaddai, shadowlands
emerging from Soraya's sword of state,
the swing vote from flower girls fluid
enough to sway Charon from ferrying
flowery Mediterranean chargés d'affaires.

60.

The charge sheet against Plautus's secret
platoon (humor on the raw putting greens,
grand guignols invalidated by no known
grandfather clause, and Soraya's ghost town
subjected to general anesthesia): drosophila
suffering Delilah's asexual delirium tremens,
creationism without an invigilating paddle,
casinos languishing in short crawl space.
Audiocassettes, au courant with gyves, give
space to dowels combining Soraya's liqueurs
with the booming of listservs on pregnant
Easter Mondays: natural magic whispers
lithium truths around the harpy maypole,
inverting scatology's second childhood.

61.

Those noble savages reciting the pledge of
allegiance, pudding faces emitting cantus
firmus known from Boolean cantinas of
bookkeeping, keep dying with their boots
on, Soraya, concrescent living deaths in
Lydian clavichords: their claustral bills of
health, claws in place, beanstalks of Anglo-
mania growing in anhydrous repose, addle
my allopatric brain. Soraya, make me an
alligator from postnuptial depression, ask
me to belch belles-lettres behind curtains
of bambino architraves, while the area
codes of archangels' eyes provide lo-fi
logarithms, sick days on prairie shikara.

62.

Late Prague Spring, bougainvillea-shrouded,
shadow play stitching ebonics with Shudra
echolocation, ebbs with the low profile of
cheatgrass in the shadowlands: Soraya, of
what road movies are you a fan, whose roar
of sleeping sickness will you sling toward
the stepparents of tetrameter? Performative
thumbnails conserve caissons of aromatic
oil. Honi soit qui mal y pense! Honeycombed
calando honor, shiatsu for irenic bayadère,
all wasted before the iron maiden's ironic
diaphragm. Spumes of Soraya's Bessemer
beginnings surround the ba gua of etymons
pointed to me by effusive eggheads this Eid.

63.

The cruel effigy we knew from Egyptology
was burnt. Yesterday the snakes chattered of
milk in the dirt-cheap baggage, chaperones taking
mantids to cellars of dirt and ash. Soraya passed
the Mantoux test like a mannequin at camp.
Camouflaged but not camera-ready, I belly-
danced my way to the caviar benchmarks,
rode the beach buggy to muzak, mussulman
in love with mustard gas. Sweet sultans grow
in the warbling aftermath of grad school, so
we can formalize, Soraya, basilisks obscured
by invaded personal space. Physician, master
of phylogeny, basso profundo echoes in your
phratry of castoffs like believers in shock.

64.

We have developed the language of Benares,
flower power for gestapo beetles, harmonic
series moving toward memorandums of blond
guns: Soraya's industrial borstals, indecent
strikes to beat back the high rollers of graffiti
fame. In the family of gourds, jinni make a
fuss over floribunda surrounding dominical
letters. (The disguise we wear is disgorged.)
Child of crusades, the gulf between birth and
musical chairs extends the running battle
so that sweet chimney sweeps alienate their
trumpet majors: visions of Soraya, trunk
call to trustees, liberation theology feeding
librettos brought to code by condottieri.

65.

Scorpioid torments at the drinking fountain,
Soraya, Gallipoli's inner space has room for
inkblot tests given by second-generation
shamuses: shantytowns in Shangri-La, unctuous
citrine civilians, musky civets clairaudient,
hors de combat, because lanterned maggids
have opened the door to magic-bullet realism.
(I sit like a card index ruined by castor oil.)
Promissory notes to the promised land come
due like sea spiders radiating poison. Sub-
montane pronuncios speak the language of
tympani bridging Type A and Type B: we
have descanted on the categorical imperative,
caterwauling like sledgehammers in pain.

66.

Appanage we provided to clinical psychology
in a climate of haram ibis hysteria, iatrogenic
hypothesis clambering for Soraya's queered
ice age, the ice buckets flowing with hansels
presented to the field of icons: identikits we
blew in the idiomatic wind, boarding musical
saws, helped us mushroom into videos of
nebular constitutionalism. Soraya, mercerized
prophylaxis, among the proper fractions I
memorized few have yielded prosaic returns:
tropism reordering christingles for bluegrass
viewability comes also as victory sign, welt-
schmerz of blue truck farms our determined
trover gave up to the werewolves of hemlock.

67.

They accuse me of being a wiccan, if not
a parody of widow's weeds darkening the
burghers of West Bengal like unrecognized
passwords. They fault me, Soraya, of being
pastoralist to arcadia's archetypical angels of
honesty, archenemy to honest women honed
by god's homosocial wit or Honecker's tunnel
of love. I am the tuning fork for steel alibis
upperclassmen love. Yoked with camelot
forebrain, singled out like force majeure after
a storm of peer reviews, pedant among cross-
ing pedestrians, I resist, Soraya, theologians
in Theodora's court, mala fide absorption
into the bubble economy of camphor trees.

68.

Compassion fatigue among metalinguists,
leathern like companion animals hanging
to the bricks of clinical death, butchery
approved by buskins sporting Cliffs Notes
to cliometrics: don't you, Soraya, lark-
felled hornbook, regret the saber saws
rattling in Averroës's cage? How does
Avalon return to the avant-garde's aviary
of figureheads? Orthotropic figurine, non
est factum custody of berets in bequeathed
orange, the disadvantage accrues only to
Soraya's dirndl skirt, unfunded skunk-
works refusing bridge money, the glow
of the sky on the run flaring as catafalque.

69.

If Bhutto went to Biafra, biased toward bi-
centennial chains, rickshaws in the middle
passage flying toward the ears of perfec-
tionism, then the prolegomenon Soraya wrote
to my regionalism would be relief itself.
Calligraphy is a dead art when call waiting
takes care of buntings planted by Buñuel
in the Bulgarian honey fungus of our minds.
Symbiosis of cecropia with ceiling-bound
moths, Soraya reeving through the rotten
boroughs as silent partner, rouge et noir
played to the end, as griffins grind out Ma
Bell's lyricism for John Does in jodhpurs,
macaroni penguins offering Job's tears.

70.

Job hunt at Kumbh Mela, kuchen or kufic
kreplach, Samarkand's glazed samba, or
saltarellos we colonists enforced after the
end of the color bar: Soraya, census of
centenarians, bench warrants written in
amnesia foretell Belshazzar's autochthon
craving. (In this land autodidacts panto-
mime the premiership of noir beta tests.)
False fruit composed of fallen pieces of
familiar lychees, liquid lonely hearts
divided by Soraya's milky mimeographs
of ethnomusicology, what is this noise
like negative equity, proof of necrophilia
among crafty women of needlework?

71.

Know-nothing sky above the knoll of sofas
and Knopf's ladies of breezes: landsmen
disabled by lancet-wielding heirs of Scipio
Africanus, Soraya's scimitar a tail of litter
and wheels. Everywhere a caulk's obstetrical
vowels, hard as obsidian sculpted like touch-
screens for those with Tourette's syndrome:
a mood of click-stop deforestation. Buckle
down, Soraya, your sweetheart neckline is
Bucephalus's temptation. We have tenancy
in common with webmasters, bustards slow
as the expansion of British India, quailing
before canasta, butlers' pantries loaded with
reserves of health food for bombed sextons.

72.

Hierophants who prowl like rock lizards
in the excipient foam of cabin-class dreams,
come at me like bubble memories of the
Byzantine empire, for I was there, Soraya,
bucolic major-domo in charge of majority
rule, malachite bearing archipelagoes of
musique concrète. Mixing the membranes
of Niflheim with nightingales of nostalgia
was ever my referred pain. Soraya, smoky
quartz smolders beneath my candid snafus,
as though I were a compass to Baluchi in
drums, violent dropsy among the plumbers
of collapse: classical ploughshares sweep
past dive-bombing Sunday divertissements.

73.

Footlocker your divining rods deflated in,
the Qur'an's raccoon rationality, forays at
eclampsia among eccentric demoiselles
demographically canceled, Soraya, inter-
marriage with the presidium of cremation
stands as rebuke to bilingual attorneys
general. The law is an attaché case of
midsummer troubles, answering machine
to our annus mirabilis. Anise-sweet
annalists, Soraya, annunciate photopic
tantrums, while I, living Tao-te-Ching,
crystal-gaze at my lost country cousins,
lately coupling with beefeaters growing
like fungus in the breakfasts of bedlam.

74.

At our bedside, an accounting of prime
cuts of beef: chateaubriand following club
steak like Beethoven's stung koans. Sex
industry bulging at contrabassoon dais
of Soraya's lingam work, line drawings
whose density is of lintels, emigrants in
steerage. This is merchandise for the
meat grinder after Greenwich Mean Time's
meconium arcana. Mirabile dictu, email
arrives like evensong or phrase book to
zero population growth: zephyr flying
past the liquidity ratios around which
protolanguage loops, like Soraya's star
of protest, tamasha of congestive failure.

75.

The congregants demand conjugal rights
as per quantity theory, as per plumage
devoted to pivotal moments in oblation:
Soraya, enlightened enneagram, graviton
to the haute bourgeoisie, ghostbusters
have come to live in the ghetto of stories,
entropy's absolute temperature is a puff-
ball of en primeur gibberish. Ingénues
prefer sorbets of songwriting ellipticity,
circumcision for tangential chakras, cer-
tiorari in Soraya's court of cerulean C-
sections. Chacun à son goût! Cro-Magnon
man, like hermaphrodite brig, is house-
mother to history's hog-tied orogeny.

76.

On a late February evening my feathered
friends descended on fahlerz glass, fecund
genies of relativity. I took the genre painting
out in the haboob, bypassing the emporium
of interruptions. Soraya's idée reçue was
that ideograms are earth's wheelchair signs
for marked-down prayer books: marquetry
among magians given to industrial espionage.
The hype about longdog idiolects is lentando
among jihadist koinonia, Soraya's war with
horse sense, when the hostages return to
Hephaestus, hidalgos free at last of the gravy
train. Even gravity is an ape with the mind of
a pencil, ghazal like crabs, mossy Spanglish.

77.

After a night among giant tortoises, I broke
through Ghirlandaio's ghost frescoes, only
a toad in gaudy Hebrew, a head of state to
gondolas from glossography's courteous
days. Soraya diffuses diglossia when we
seven sisters blow the cortège in the set
piece to cosmopolis's irony: criterium our
crinky parents criticized for the sake of
incest as ideogram. The mind as idiot board
awakens a crisis of miles of music, froideur
between Soraya's frontispiece to holiday
camp and the formularies of gear ratios.
I borrow the flag of convenience after
fiat money ends the ibex dinner dance.

78.

I grew up with mattock aimed at millibars
of empressement, employability among
earth mothers who lived next door to my
dodo doctorate in docudrama. Labefaction
comes as cheerleaders in Chinese boxes,
Soraya's contact sheet humbled by the
Cultural Revolution in error. Curb market
for curriculums in costume dramas has
indigenized couch potatoes diagramed like
Indian summer for ladybugs and lavender
cotton. Soraya's lava flow swallows the
laureates of laughing gas, leviathan not
fitting into any known fiscal year, fissures
opening up in garrisons of immunization.

79.

That was a greeting card for greyhounds
caught in the Gregorian calendar, green
fee our Gresham's Law knew nothing
about: Soraya as go-go futurologist at
peace in the fourth estate's funhouse is
as distillated as fragile X syndrome. So
don't trespass the fosse along empyrean
spirit lamps, we are flannel for earflaps.
I dream of the gawky Gatling gun, mash
note you sent me, Soraya, after the masque
ended on a note of purpure masjids, the
purlieu around the FTSE index color-
coded for my cane-chair candidacy:
heredity brings forth ice-cold hepcats.

80.

The fields of Iceland spar, as maladjusted
as the I Ching, make-work leechcraft to
end the legal fiction whereby I holiday in
your jujube craft: Soraya, jacquerie we
performed upon leaving Rumi's jailhouse
has come back to haunt knitting-machine
dreams. All I know is Leda's learned
helplessness, Key Largo's kilobits of
ketene IP addresses. Ipsissima verba
League of Nations poison, glass free of
economic indicators, Soraya's recitative
recollection of codes of sickness, and
shuttle diplomacy our soigné imitation of
the valetudinarian spandex squirearchy.

81.

Illuminati's hyperfocal distance, hog-wild
about Iphigenia's fortnight with Fortran,
fortepiano gamete, the cycle of Soraya's
galvanic skin response under no stress of
Ibn Saud's Hippocrene spam: in vivo or
Library of Congress's flouncy libertarian
hegemony, either way we are hermetic
hand tools in the militia's milk parlor.
War is a mild midwinter migraine, speech
therapy for spasmophile revolutionaries
in Sparta's pay. Soraya's fumarole geom-
etries of gentile sightseeing never end in
Sindhi chapels of matte sisterhood, past
siroccos stoked by deism's distress sale.

82.

In the twilight of monosomy, Masson taught
automatic drawing, mass-produced tears of
the mater dolorosa entering slot machines in
electric arcades: you were there, Soraya,
wearing the anti-pope's mandarin jacket, an-
Najaf's animism a mariage blanc as official
as marsh Arabs in decline. The panchayat in
recess compiles pandects on stipends of
confidence. Degrees of Sassanian douceur
de vivre infect the eagles above our hamlet
on Shabbos: signet ring bleeding slavery's
slasher film, Soraya's soprano spadework,
tularemia transmitted to visiting professors
of logophile vivisection, all of it exposed.

83.

The locus classicus of frottage is the Revised
Standard Version's silviculture for fractured
eyes: no, Soraya, eat bread pudding, seventh
wonder of the world. Sevastopol's challah
emissaries stitch cardboards of respiratory
numbers, each carbon cycle as virtuous as
Piltdown man in the Pine Tree State. Stroke
play behind the bamboo curtain occupies no
little bandwidth. The audience at the auction
sits like the ancien régime soaking hyperbole
from inferiors, Soraya's stablemates tattling
like table dancers, besieged tautonyms black
as the insides of walnuts: benzine binary code
operating upon numbed surfaced benthos.

84.

How is it like to achieve suffrage among
tanned leaves of Sudan grass, your success
story tour en l'air, unipotent, uninvoked,
candescent like bottleneck guitar, Botticelli
pinning coronets on corpsmen? Soraya's de-
coupage for trebuchets is treacherous like the
seven-year itch, creeping past the travesties
of decameter, dendriform bodies pooled at
the head of the Ponzi scheme. Poor box we
passed at the bodhi tree, Soraya, shutting the
stable door after the gossip was gossamer,
collected sfumato accumulating around
regime change, regrouped dialects of our
childhood registered like invented moss.

85.

Dying is interpreted in the jiggered reign
of terror as something akin to rehearsal, revue
for the Thirty Years' War, Tibetan antelope
uncolored like thymine, uranium sprawling
like urban forest in upstart video surgery:
Soraya, victory garden for the viridescent
virtual community, become visible when
you go to war, the waltz of the wanderjahr
is condemned to dramaturgy. Your counsel
on the appropriate drawdown, Soraya? How
does the Edinburgh Festival educate eight
minutes in the Florida room? Florescent
debt is frantic like frangipani worth less
than sixpence, climbing past social realism.

86.

Sobriety, as late-glacial as soca, your klaxon
Latin lovers are knight errants I found on
the edge of pseudonyms. Psychic income
generated from Imhotep's imagined prunella
hyperspace is thick as the hedgerow around
jacinth invention. Metropole of metaphor,
Soraya, magenta mushroom in the looking
glass, will the ligature hold in lebensraum?
How do we go about undoing leatherwork
in the kampong of homicide? Kabuki jurists
free Soraya's interpellators of housekeeping
discourse: do you know any hagiologists in
Gropius's grotto? How do we make doves
from glass, send gravid lovers to the reefs?

87.

Gouache whose academic status, like gowns
of governable grace, resists hyphenation: I
like, Soraya, to be the interim nerve, loose
angle of isometric freedom. Indirect rule at
the legal clinic arose like majuscules of
tranquility, the majlis of arcana adjourning
just when the makeovers were no longer
brief. The nobility rots like metal at the O.K.
Corral, sheepdogs on oil platforms. Pastorale
conducted in old money's sapiential foundry
reduces me to a branch of patristics. Fouetté
I mastered, everlasting peccary at peasant
revolts, makes me, Soraya, a commoner, co-
author as underplayed as cockatrice in pain.

88.

Days of bushcraft, days of poet laureates
shooting turtles in bookmobiles: rebel yell
for digital cash, differentia we compressed,
Soraya, in the cere dampness of the customs
house. I am contour feather at the last tank
town on the tango route, I think the third eye
is a French letter when not a pastry freeze-
framed in the exosphere of wired elections.
Electric eels reproduce the music of shock.
Desaparecidos, cubist-boned, appear in the
crack house like open-faced desk magnets.
Soraya, opera seria in cloak of toponyms,
travertine joy took me by surprise at the
sovereign poles, I was hedgehog's height.

89.

Space warp. Please. Sowetos of the tough-
minded tourist class. Enrobed in snares of
DNA profiling. Live dobby weaves of gift-
ware. Dioramas through which individualism
disappears. Soraya, Indian file, insignia of
the narrativized layabout. Nargileh drawing
naphthene to the bones of Sinhalese spokes-
persons. Splenetic plutocracy dancing the
can-can on chairs of displeasure. Bravissimo,
Soraya, the bread-and-butter letter came just
when I gave tea to the blackshirts. Thalassic
fault in visas. Is it typhus? Clouds of variety
meats. Vulva-coded gentile dysphasia, suet
of ten commandments for canine distemper.

90.

Do you know the right color temperature
to make Colorado and its pathetic fallacy
transparent? Who is patently on our candid
sunbathing side? Visions of sump in which,
Soraya, alienated from the solstice of weight,
the fovea at last perceives the femme fatale,
Fata Morgana in the fat city. Fatimid end-
paper is as good as effleurage to my face.
Soraya (delta rhythms free like cucumber
mosaic) why is sleep our costume of pairing?
In the councils of mutism, the muzhiks'
nausea is nugget of the nuclear age proven
like pseudorabies: rainfall on raking light,
the raised beach at the end of the rainbow.

91.

I have tried to rebut rebirthing in my lucid
moments. They wear rebozos to pronounce
the mujahideen as nothing but monthlong
memorabilia, lowbrow mandarins. Soraya,
the lithograph (living out of the litigious
suitcase) of mawkish mayapples may yet
mature into a useful road sign: sand castle
on which robin redbreasts alight like bifid
samurai. Sessile sestinas, dreamcatchers'
dragnet between time and earth, Soraya,
be the damselfish of crépon, backstroke to
Daphnis's back-to-nature invention: and
I will not be au courant in the auditorium
where atlas moths suffocate from heat.

92.

What is cerebral dominance? The ginger-
bread bank, to which the helots come hop-
scotching, is ingravescent lambada, only
laminate for Kronos: Soraya, is your belt-
tightening as awakened as Avogadro's
Law? I agree, concrete universals can be
concupiscent if not watched like deer.
I fade like the decrescendo of deep brain
stimulation. Among the instrumentation
associated with pulsating keiretsu: in-
oculum for inquisitors general, late hours
in the house church, gunpowder falling
on stony ground, Soraya's atonal atlas
of reliable dipsomania, seasick regimen.

93.

Infidel, burn the self-portrait, discipline's
mutilation (siltstone in your pond of sleep)
blows a hole in holiness: whenever Soraya
goes busting the guildhall (the gentlemen's
agreement keeping gold in the equator,
the school board benefiting bondswomen),
then bon vivants in the osseous new econ-
omy come out of newsprint, teach lessons
in ataxia. I love the atmospherics of the
Ashmolean Museum, aside from cobra
shame and arithmetic of Ariel's armature.
We leave the armed camp to the mercy
of reliable prosopopeia, and protagonists
inaugurate the Moulin Rouge for Soraya.

94.

This last mountain chain, dotted with blue-crowned motmots, or did you mean the julep jumping-off point for déclassé inseminators? I inquire, Soraya, on behalf of organic lexemes. Upon levying the heftiest serialism in our section of taedium vitae, suddenly the taffeta rugs splinter to tabors from the next block. The discography of the daisy chain is hardly countrified: cinephiles in Soraya's circumference waste their beaux gestes over glimpses of soma. How will we sing of tight money turning us into tribes of trichinae? How will the glyphs be gnostic as moths floundering over alarms of light?

95.

The people of cornbread, contemporaries
fighting continental drift, lipogrammatic
experiments in litany's main clause: do
you know what it is to be the black-billed
magpie in Soraya's melody of Mithraism?
This is a black-and-white mix-up: black
flag at the montessori door, as avid as
Monument Valley lit up by mooncalves.
I was there—or not—skirt-chasing Calig-
ula's leftovers, dressed in calico as blue
as the bloom of Bloomsbury. Inching
through incest's incognito knotting, I
mark Soraya's lex talonis, never heard
from since levanters evicted meaning.

96.

You call me lotus-eater supplanting love-
in-a-mist hand puppets? Ideas of infinity
throw themselves at me when I teleport
your presence as a study in poker. Not
to mention never having been the ne plus
ultra of nepotism, only the nerve trunk
theorized by contumacy. Only Soraya
knows my crinoline desperation to whirl
with the eddy. It was an edge city for the
worship of yohimbine we reached, zeugma
stiff as aqua regia. Is the versal letter at
the beginning of the last chapter Soraya's
whetstone, windward like wisdom lit-
erature, or just a trembling theomachy?

97.

We are slow as theorems in travelogues
populated by blind car bombs: courtship
of the dramatis personae on Menander's
loading dock is Soraya's cue to bank
on jurassic second sight. I was a reader
in good faith, my synthesis was choppy,
but only on schooldays in my smudged
birthplace. That bawdy house for tantric
rainbow coalitions? Dear eschatology,
do not cheat me of neutral espionage. I
am not the netherworld you have noted
in panhandles of panic. I am Soraya's
fornax logic, freemartin taking my own
life to pack the style sheet in a suitcase.

98.

The bustle we heard on the way out, of
course it's what bushwhacking ends in,
Christian names as lively as chow mein,
the gap between Coltrane and free jazz,
effable gaia singing to the greyhounds.
I lost my black book in the columbarium,
Soraya, at last stranded like a Moorish
fantasy, nothing more than folk memory.
They came bearing empires of poison,
and I had no choice but to be ikebana
in someone else's interior monologue:
lexic for method acting, Soraya, phago-
cyte on the loose, petroglyph to whom
Proteus replied, which was all the time.

99.

They say the muse's light touch is best:
I prefer Erato when I can murmur her
name, but who is to say Polyhymnia is
not really the outspoken fountain whose
rank I fumble toward in the spindly dark?
The schizoid's POV, flamboyant like
nostalgia for full employment, haunts
me, Soraya, like derecho over fauvist
inventions. All that is done has been
thought by Kilimanjaro, the mother
country is a moss animal, as we both
know, Soraya, as golden as the neck-
lace around pandemonium: came the
nuit blanche finding me dead opossum.

100.

Farewell is a deadly sin, belladonna in
the fingers of exactitude, so the rote
prime ministers of feathering put on
tattered stockings, just because. Taut
Soraya in the threadbare crystalline
sphere is an anomaly only as long as
the telegraph keeps glowing: past that,
the reverie turns interdenominational.
Let the interim suppositions play out
in the maisonette as trespassed as toy
cinnabar, the wheel of Soraya having
come full circle in sprinkled santeria,
a language we speak in swells of silk,
a sweetheart of an unhurried tattletale.

ANIS SHIVANI is the author of several critically acclaimed books of fiction, poetry, and criticism, including *Anatolia and Other Stories* (2009), *Against the Workshop* (2011), *The Fifth Lash and Other Stories* (2012), *My Tranquil War and Other Poems* (2012), and *Karachi Raj: A Novel* (2015). Both *Anatolia and Other Stories* and *The Fifth Lash and Other Stories* were longlisted for the Frank O'Connor international short story award. Books in progress or recently finished include *Literature in an Age of Globalization, Death is a Festival: Poems, Plastic Realism: Neoliberalism in Recent American Fiction*, and the novels *A History of the Cat in Nine Chapters or Less, Abruzzi, 1936*, and *An Idiot's Guide to America*. Anis's work appears in the *Yale Review, Georgia Review, Boston Review, Iowa Review, Threepenny Review, Michigan Quarterly Review, Antioch Review, Southwest Review, Prairie Schooner, AGNI, Fence, Epoch, Boulevard, Pleiades, Denver Quarterly, Verse, Colorado Review, Quarterly West, New Letters, Subtropics, Times Literary Supplement, London Magazine, Meanjin, Fiddlehead*, and other leading literary journals. His criticism appears widely in newspapers and magazines such as *Salon, Huffington Post, Daily Beast, In These Times, Texas Observer, San Francisco Chronicle, Boston Globe, Austin American-Statesman, Kansas City Star, Pittsburgh Post-Gazette, St. Petersburg Times, Charlotte Observer*, and many other outlets. Anis is the winner of a 2012 Pushcart Prize, graduated from Harvard College, and lives in Houston, Texas.

TITLES FROM BLACK WIDOW PRESS
TRANSLATION SERIES

A Life of Poems, Poems of a Life
by Anna de Noailles. Translated by Norman
R. Shapiro. Introduction by Catherine Perry.

Approximate Man and Other Writings
by Tristan Tzara. Translated and edited by
Mary Ann Caws.

Art Poétique
by Guillevic. Translated by Maureen Smith.

The Big Game by Benjamin Péret.
Translated with an introduction by
Marilyn Kallet.

Boris Vian Invents Boris Vian:
A Boris Vian Reader.
Edited and translated by Julia Older.

Capital of Pain by Paul Eluard.
Translated by Mary Ann Caws, Patricia Terry,
and Nancy Kline.

Chanson Dada: Selected Poems
by Tristan Tzara. Translated with an
introduction and essay by Lee Harwood.

Essential Poems and Writings of Joyce Mansour:
A Bilingual Anthology. Translated with an
introduction by Serge Gavronsky.

Essential Poems and Prose of Jules Laforgue.
Translated and edited by Patricia Terry.

Essential Poems and Writings of Robert Desnos:
A Bilingual Anthology. Edited with an
introduction and essay by Mary Ann Caws.

EyeSeas (Les Ziaux) by Raymond Queneau.
Translated with an introduction by
Daniela Hurezanu and Stephen Kessler.

Fables in a Modern Key by Pierre Coran.
Edited and translated by Norman R. Shapiro.
Full-color illustrations by Olga Pastuchiv.

Forbidden Pleasures: New Selected Poems
[1924–1949] by Luis Cernuda.
Translated by Stephen Kessler.

Furor and Mystery & Other Writings
by René Char. Edited and translated by
Mary Ann Caws and Nancy Kline.

Guarding the Air:
Selected Poems of Gunnar Harding.
Translated and edited by Roger Greenwald.

The Inventor of Love & Other Writings
by Gherasim Luca. Translated by Julian & Laura
Semilian. Introduction by Andrei Codrescu.
Essay by Petre Răileanu.

Jules Supervielle: Selected Prose and Poetry.
Translated by Nancy Kline and Patricia Terry.

La Fontaine's Bawdy by Jean de La Fontaine.
Translated with an introduction by
Norman R. Shapiro.

Last Love Poems of Paul Eluard. Translated
with an introduction by Marilyn Kallet.

Love, Poetry (L'amour la poésie) by Paul Eluard.
Translated with an essay by Stuart Kendall.

Pierre Reverdy: Poems, Early to Late. Translated
by Mary Ann Caws and Patricia Terry.

Poems of André Breton: A Bilingual Anthology.
Translated with essays by Jean-Pierre Cauvin
and Mary Ann Caws.

Poems of A.O. Barnabooth by Valery Larbaud.
Translated by Ron Padgett and Bill Zavatsky.

Poems of Consummation by Vicente Aleixandre.
Translated by Stephen Kessler.

Préversities: A Jacques Prévert Sampler.
Translated and edited by Norman R. Shapiro.

The Sea and Other Poems by Guillevic.
Translated by Patricia Terry. Introduction
by Monique Chefdor.

To Speak, to Tell You? Poems by Sabine Sicaud.
Translated by Norman R. Shapiro. Introduction
and notes by Odile Ayral-Clause.

Forthcoming Translations

Earthlight (Clair de Terre) by André Breton.
Translated by Bill Zavatsky and Zack Rogrow.
(New and revised edition.)

The Gentle Genius of Cécile Périn:
Selected Poems (1906–1956).
Edited and translated by Norman R. Shapiro.

WWW.BLACKWIDOWPRESS.COM